PUERTO RICO

the people and culture

Erinn Banting

A Bobbie Kalman Book

The Lands, Peoples, and Cultures Series

Crabtree Publishing Company

www.crabtreebooks.com

The Lands, Peoples, and Cultures Series

Created by Bobbie Kalman

Coordinating editor
Ellen Rodger

Production coordinator
Rosie Gowsell

Project development, photo research, design, and editing
First Folio Resource Group, Inc.
  Erinn Banting
  Tom Dart
  Alana Lai
  Claire Milne
  Jaimie Nathan
  Debbie Smith

Prepress and printing
Worzalla Publishing Company

Consultants
Ruth Burgos-Sasscer, Ph.D., Houston Community College
System; Manuel Hernandez, Latino Literature Consultant
Pan American Cultural Exchange, Houston

Photographs
AP/Wide World Photos: p. 24 (left); Tony Arruza: p. 16
(bottom), p. 23 (top); Bettmann/Corbis/Magma: p. 9 (both),
p. 10 (top), p. 25 (top); Corbis Sygma/Magma: p. 29 (bottom);
Marc Crabtree: cover, p. 11 (top), p. 17 (right), p. 27, p. 30;
Peter Crabtree: title page, p. 12 (right), p. 16 (top), p. 25
(bottom), p. 22 (bottom), p. 26; Robert Fried/D. Donne Bryant
Stock: p. 31 (top); Jeremy Horner/Corbis/Magma: p. 10
(bottom); Len Kaufman: p. 7 (right), p. 13 (right), p. 22 (right);
Bob Krist/Corbis/Magma: p. 19 (bottom);
Erich Lessing/Art Resource: p. 21 (right); Stephanie
Maze/Corbis/Magma: p. 6, p. 13 (left), p. 14; Suzanne
Murphy-Larronde/D. Donne Bryant Stock: p. 12 (left), p. 15
(both), p. 17 (left), p. 18, p. 19 (top), p. 23 (bottom), p. 24 (right),
p. 28, p. 29 (top left), p. 31 (bottom); North Wind Pictures: p. 8;
Gianni Dagli Orti/Corbis/Magma: p. 7 (left); Reuters
NewMedia Inc./Corbis/Magma: p. 11 (bottom),
p. 20 (right); Royalty-free/Corbis/Magma: p. 3; J. B.
Russell/Corbis/Magma: p. 20 (left); Smithsonian American
Art Museum, Washington DC/Art Resource: p. 21 (left);
Frank Trapper/Corbis/Magma: p. 29 (top right)

Illustrations
Dianne Eastman: icon
David Wysotski, Allure Illustrations: back cover
Ben Hodson: pp. 4–5

Cover: A boy in uniform stops to chat with friends on his way
home from a day at school.

Icon: *Vejigante* masks, which appear at the head of each
section, are worn at different festivals throughout Puerto Rico.
The masks are made from coconuts or gourds covered in clay
or papier-mâché. Traditionally, the masks were made to look
like frightening devils, but today they also look like people
and animals.

Title page: A singer performs in traditional costume before a
crowd at a regional agricultural festival.

Back cover: The *coquí* is a tiny frog that lives in forested areas
all over Puerto Rico. The frog is named after the musical call it
makes each evening.

Published by
Crabtree Publishing Company

PMB 16A,
350 Fifth Avenue
Suite 3308
New York
N.Y. 10118

612 Welland Avenue
St. Catharines
Ontario, Canada
L2M 5V6

73 Lime Walk
Headington
Oxford OX3 7AD
United Kingdom

Cataloging-in-publication data
Banting, Erinn.
    Puerto Rico. The people and culture / Erinn Banting.
    p. cm. -- (Lands, peoples, and cultures)
Includes index.
Summary: Introduces the history, religions, holidays and festivals,
arts, sports, languages, and literature of Puerto Rico.
    ISBN 0-7787-9334-6 (RLB) -- ISBN 0-7787-9702-3 (PB)
    1. Puerto Rico--Social life and customs--Juvenile literature. 2.
Puerto Rico--History--Juvenile literature. [1. Puerto Rico--Social life
and customs. 2. Puerto Rico--History.] I. Title: People and culture.
II. Title. III. Series: Lands, peoples, and cultures.
    F1960.B36 2003
    972.95--dc21
                                                    2003001269
                                                    LC

Contents

A Taíno myth

Thousands of years ago, the island of Puerto Rico was called Boriquén. Boriquén means "Land of the Brave Lord" in the language of the Taíno, one of the first peoples to live in Puerto Rico. In Taíno villages, families gathered to tell stories about their heroes, about magic, and about how the world began. The story of the golden flower tells how the island of Boriquén came to be.

The golden flower

There was no water when the world began. Only a single, **barren** mountain stood in the middle of a desert **plain**. People lived on top of the mountain, but they had very little food.

One day, a boy went for a walk on the plain to search for something to eat. He noticed a small seed floating by and put it in his pouch.

Each day as he walked, the boy found a new seed. Soon, his pouch was full. "I will plant these seeds on top of the mountain and see what becomes of them," he said to himself.

After several days, a tiny green sprout popped out of the ground where the boy had planted the seeds. The next day, colorful flowers appeared; the day after that, thick plants; and the day after that, majestic trees. Soon, a forest covered the mountain.

In the middle of the forest was a beautiful golden flower growing from a vine, and a golden globe growing from the flower. The globe shone as brightly as the sun, but something unusual was happening inside.

"Listen," a woman said. "You can hear strange murmurs and curious sounds inside the globe." People were scared, so they decided to stay away from the globe.

In the meantime, two men living on the desert plain each decided that they would like to own the shining globe. Imagine the power they could have! They could make the world light or dark at their command.

The two men climbed the mountain, one on one side of the peak and one on the other. They reached the top at the same time, only to realize that the globe was not the sun, as they had thought. It was a *calabaza*, or pumpkin.

Both men wanted the *calabaza* for themselves. They began to kick and tug at the vine until it broke. The *calabaza* rolled down the mountain faster and faster until it smashed into a rock.

Giant waves of water poured out of the *calabaza*, followed by whales, dolphins, crabs, and sunfish. The waters flooded the desert plain and climbed the sides of the mountain, stopping only when they reached the edge of the forest that the boy had planted.

When the people on top of the mountain peeked their heads out of the trees where they were hiding, they saw small streams trickling through the forest and a vast sea stretching out below. Their mountain was now an island home.

"The sea was hiding in the *calabaza*!" the people cried. "With all this water, we can feed our crops and fish for food. We will never be hungry again!"

The little boy looked out at the sea below and smiled. He was happy that water had come to the earth.

Early history

Some historians believe that the first Puerto Ricans came from South America 4,000 years ago. They paddled across the Caribbean Sea in log boats or canoes and settled on the southern coast. They survived by fishing, gathering food, and hunting with tools made from bones, shells, and stones. The Archaics, or los Arcaicos, arrived from present-day Florida between 2,000 and 4,000 years ago. They lived along the northern coast where they fished and gathered clams and oysters. The Arawak peoples began to arrive on the island around 2,000 years ago. They hunted, gathered food, and grew sweet potatoes, corn, and other crops they brought from South America.

The Taíno

The Taíno, an Arawak people, came by boat between 600 A.D. and 1000 A.D. They built *bohíos*, or wooden homes with grass roofs, in villages called *yucayeques*. At the center of each village was a *plaza* where meetings were held. *Plazas* were also used for celebrations, military practices, and a fast-paced ball game called *batey*. Surrounding the villages was farmland where the Taíno grew tobacco, corn, pineapples, **manioc**, and sweet potatoes. Life for the Taíno was peaceful, except when the Carib, a group of peoples from South America, attacked Taíno settlements.

Other arrivals

Italian explorer Christopher Columbus landed on Puerto Rico in 1493. He claimed the island for Spain, the country that paid for his exploration, and changed its name from Boriquén to San Juan Bautista, or Saint John the Baptist. In 1508, Spain sent its first **colonists** to the island, led by another explorer, Juan Ponce de León. The colonists established a settlement in the northeast called Caparra, and Ponce de León was named the first Spanish governor of San Juan Bautista.

(top) Large stone slabs decorated with carvings surround the oval-shaped plaza at the Caguana Indian Ceremonial Park in Utuado, a town in central Puerto Rico. Archaeologists believe the carvings represent Taíno gods and goddesses or important village leaders.

Many Carib, who were enemies of the Spanish colonists, were caught during battles and forced into slavery. In this illustration, a Carib slave cuts the leaves off a sugar cane stem.

Slavery

The Spanish soon discovered that their new land had an abundance of gold and rich soil ideal for growing sugar cane, coffee, and tobacco. They forced the Taíno to work in mines and on **plantations** as slaves. Many Taíno committed suicide, rebelled, or joined their former enemies, the Carib, on neighboring islands or in Puerto Rico's mountains. Most of those who remained in slavery died from starvation, overwork, or diseases that the Spanish brought. Within years, the estimated 30,000 to 40,000 Taíno who lived on the island when the Spanish arrived were almost completely wiped out. More workers were needed, so in 1518, the Spanish government began to send slaves to Puerto Rico from West Africa.

A new settlement

By 1521, Juan Ponce de León had moved the inhabitants of Caparra farther west. They settled on the shores of a bay that was easier to defend against Carib attacks and that was protected from storms coming across the Atlantic Ocean. The bay quickly became the busiest port in the Caribbean and was given the name Puerto Rico, or "Rich Port." Eventually, the names of the port and the island were switched. The port became known as San Juan, while the island became Puerto Rico.

Defending San Juan

Many countries wanted to gain control of Puerto Rico. Its central location in the Caribbean Sea made it an ideal base for Spain's enemies, such as Britain and Holland, to attack Spanish colonies in the Caribbean and South America. Puerto Rico was also an important stop on many trade routes. Sailors on ships carrying gold, silver, pearls, and other riches rested there and refilled their stocks of food. Pirates were eager to steal these riches and used Puerto Rico as a base from which to raid ships. Settlers built **fortifications** to protect San Juan from invasions, but this did not stop the invaders.

Construction of El Morro, a fortress with six levels, began in 1539. The fortress was attacked by the British in 1595 and again in 1598. In 1625, the Dutch attacked El Morro and burned down much of San Juan.

Pirates

Puerto Rico was the perfect place for pirates from countries such as Britain and Spain to hide, rest, stock up on supplies, and conceal the goods that they stole. Many pirates hid their treasures in caves in the 200-foot (60-meter) cliffs surrounding Mona Island. Some Puerto Ricans believe that there is still treasure in those caves.

Puerto Rico also had its own pirates. Many robbed ships on the high seas because their Spanish rulers did not allow them to trade legally with other Caribbean islands. The best known Puerto Rican pirate was Roberto Cofresí (1791–1825). He and his fierce crew kept many of the riches that they stole, but they also gave some to their friends and to the poor. Cofresí quickly became a hero for helping those in need. In 1824, Cofresí and his crew raided an American ship. They were captured after a vicious battle and put to death in 1825. Many Puerto Ricans still consider Cofresí a hero.

Pirates attack and burn a British ship off the coast of Puerto Rico.

Illegal trade

Through the 1700s and 1800s, Puerto Ricans became increasingly unhappy with Spanish rule. Most Puerto Ricans were forced to work on plantations that the Spanish owned. Puerto Ricans who did own land had to pay high taxes and were not allowed to trade their goods with countries other than Spain. Many people began to demand more independence from Spain, better conditions for Puerto Rico's poor people, and an end to slavery. As a result of the protests, Spain allowed Puerto Ricans to trade with other islands in the Caribbean and they lowered taxes, but they did not give up control of Puerto Rico or abolish slavery.

Rebellion

On September 23, 1868, between 600 and 1,000 rebels seeking independence from Spain captured the western town of Lares in what is called *El Grito de Lares*, or "the Shout of Lares." They declared Puerto Rico a **republic**, chose a president, and promised freedom to any slaves who joined them. The next day, the rebels marched to the neighboring town of San Sebastian, where Spanish soldiers were waiting for them. Hundreds of rebels were killed or taken prisoner, but the rebellion was not a complete failure. Puerto Ricans were granted more freedoms, including the right to organize political parties, and by 1873, slavery was abolished.

After slavery

Conditions for former slaves did not immediately improve after slavery was abolished. Many were forced to continue working on the same plantations as before, and were paid very little for their labor. Other former slaves suffered from **discrimination**, and had difficulty finding new jobs and places to live. In some areas, such as Ponce, groups of ex-slaves began their own communities, but their living conditions were very poor. They did not have proper homes, health care, or nutritious food; and many died from a deadly disease called cholera, which people get from infected food and water.

Spain finally granted Puerto Rico the right to govern itself in 1897. Luis Muñoz Rivera, a writer and politician, headed the government that took power in July 1898. Several days later, the United States invaded Puerto Rico.

The United States' invasion

United States forces arrived at Guánica Bay, in the southwest, on July 25, 1898 during a war between Spain and the United States called the Spanish-American War. The war began when the United States became involved in Cuba's fight for independence from Spain. After the Spanish-American War ended on December 10, 1898, the United States continued to occupy Puerto Rico. The military rule lasted until 1900, when the United States passed a law, called the Foraker Act, that put a council made up mostly of Americans in charge of Puerto Rico. Puerto Ricans chose their own Assembly, but members of the assembly had little real power.

American troops hide from Spanish soldiers in San Juan Creek, in this photograph from the Spanish-American War taken in 1898.

Increasing resentment

Puerto Ricans resented the fact that they were not given more control of their country, even though the United States lowered taxes and built new schools, hospitals, roads, dams, and sewage systems. Puerto Ricans were especially angry that the United States refused to grant them citizenship. After many years of protest, another law, called the Jones Act, was passed. It gave Puerto Rico greater power to elect its government and granted Puerto Ricans American citizenship.

A crowd in San Juan gathers to watch soldiers in a parade, in a 1923 celebration to welcome a new governor-general. The governor-general was the United States' main representative in Puerto Rico.

Fight for independence

A worldwide **economic** crisis known as the Great Depression and damage caused by a hurricane severely hurt Puerto Rico's economy in the 1930s. Puerto Ricans were angered by the United States' lack of help, and they demanded their independence again. **Nationalist** groups protested against American rule. One group, the Nationalist Party, held a parade to support its cause on March 21, 1937, in the southern city of Ponce. The group did not have permission for the parade, and fighting broke out between the nationalists and the police. Twenty-two people were killed and 120 were wounded. The event came to be known as the Ponce Massacre.

Luis Muñoz Marín worked hard to improve life in Puerto Rico. He fought for more independence from the United States, and tried to improve conditions for poor people.

Luis Muñoz Marín

Luis Muñoz Marín, the son of Luis Muñoz Rivera, formed a political party called the Partido Popular Democrático, or Popular Democratic Party (PDP), in 1938. As head of the PDP, Muñoz Marín helped establish Operation Bootstrap, a program designed to improve Puerto Rico's economy by encouraging foreign companies, especially American companies, to open factories on the island. Muñoz Marín also helped Puerto Rico gain more political independence. In 1946, the United States named Jesús T. Piñero the first Puerto Rican governor. The following year, Puerto Ricans were granted the right to elect their own governor. The people chose Luis Muñoz Marín.

Creation of a commonwealth

In 1951, Puerto Rico voted to become a commonwealth of the United States. As members of a commonwealth, Puerto Ricans wrote their own constitution and elected their own **legislature**, but the United States still controlled the island's relations with other countries. Puerto Ricans remained U.S. citizens, but they could not vote for the United States president. On the other hand, they did not have to pay taxes to the United States. The country's economy continued to grow under Operation Bootstrap, but many people were still unemployed. Tens of thousands of Puerto Ricans moved to New York City in search of jobs. Over time, Puerto Ricans also established large communities in New Jersey, Massachusetts, Illinois, Florida, and California. These communities are still strong today.

Operation Bootstrap brought many changes to Puerto Rico. Countries such as the United States began building factories there, and many jobs were created for Puerto Rican people.

University students meet to discuss Puerto Rican politics. Some students believe that Puerto Rico should join the United States, while others think that Puerto Rico should be totally independent.

Independence

For years, Puerto Ricans have debated about whether their country should be completely independent, remain a commonwealth, or become the 51st state of the United States. Those who want independence are afraid of losing their Spanish heritage. Those who wish to remain a commonwealth or become an American state think that Puerto Rico's connection with the United States helps the island's economy. In addition, people who would like Puerto Rico to become a state want to elect representatives to Congress and vote for the president, although they know they would have to pay high taxes to the United States.

Votes, such as one that took place in 1998, show that Puerto Ricans are unsure about what they want their status to be. In that vote, 50 percent of Puerto Ricans said that they did not want any of the options available to them — independence, statehood, or commonwealth status.

Vieques

Puerto Ricans are also concerned about the tiny island of Vieques, off the eastern coast of Puerto Rico. Three-quarters of Vieques is home to a large American naval reserve, where military drills are held. The accidental killing of a security guard during a bomb drill in 1999, as well as the increased risk of cancer and damage to the environment caused by lead and mercury in the bombs, have led many Puerto Ricans to demand that the United States Navy leave Vieques.

Protestors demonstrate against the use of Vieques for military drills, in this photograph from 2001.

Puerto Ricans' religion, like their history and culture, has been influenced by many groups, especially by the Taíno and West Africans. The Taíno believed that everything in the world, including trees, rocks, and the sky, had a spirit. The creator of the world, who gave everything a spirit, was Yuquiyú. Jurakan was an evil spirit who acted against Yuquiyú by using nature to harm people. The word "hurricane" comes from his name.

West African beliefs

Like the Taíno, West Africans believe that nature is made up of spirits. They call these spirits *orishas*. Chango is the *orisha* of fire, thunder, and lightning. Many Puerto Ricans have statues of him in their homes and **altars** where they offer him wine, fruit, and other gifts. The belief in faith healers, or people who cure illnesses by praying and performing miracles, is another important part of West African beliefs.

The Taíno worshiped lesser gods, called cemi, *as well as worshiping Yuquiyú, the creator of the world. They placed stone or wood carvings of the* cemi *in their homes and buried the carvings with them when they died.*

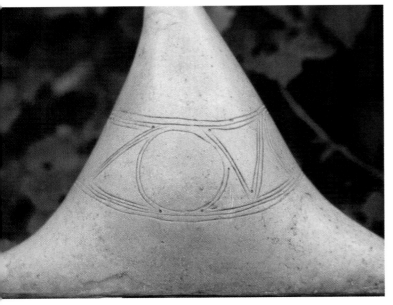

A mother brings her daughter to a Roman Catholic church in San Juan.

Christianity and Roman Catholicism

The Spanish brought their religion, Roman Catholicism, to Puerto Rico. Today, it is the country's main religion. Roman Catholicism is a **denomination** of Christianity. Christians believe in one God and in Jesus Christ, the son of God on earth. The teachings of Jesus Christ are written in a holy book called the New Testament.

Protestantism

In the 1800s, many Puerto Ricans began to follow another denomination of Christianity called Protestantism. Like other Christians, Protestants believe in God and Jesus, but some of their ideas differ. For example, Protestantism teaches that people are rewarded on earth for their good behavior and hard work. Roman Catholics believe that people are rewarded for their good deeds after they die and go to heaven. The Protestant Church broke into many sects, or groups, such as the Jehovah's Witnesses, Mormons, Methodists, Episcopalians, and Baptists. Many Puerto Ricans now follow these religions.

Alternative churches

Many people in Puerto Rico belong to religious movements that do not follow strictly traditional beliefs. One such movement is the MITA congregation. A woman named Mita founded this congregation because she wanted to help poor people in her country. In addition to holding church services, MITA owns and operates grocery stores, department stores, furniture stores, and other businesses for its members. It also provides housing and jobs to those in need. Mita died in 1970, but her church continues in many countries, including Puerto Rico, Costa Rica, Ecuador, and the United States.

Shops called botánica *sell herbs used to make medicines, as well as candles, incense, charms, and amulets, which are believed to have healing powers. People use mortars and pestles, like the ones this woman is selling, to grind the herbs and mix them together.*

Espiritismo

Espiritismo, or spiritualism, combines indigenous beliefs, like those of the Taíno, with West African and Christian beliefs and a French philosophy called **Kardecism.** Followers of *espiritismo* believe that mediums can communicate with *jípia*, or spirits of the dead. Puerto Ricans perform **rituals** to attract good spirits and to get rid of bad ones. For example, many people place bowls of fruit on their kitchen tables to keep *jípia* happy. On New Year's Eve, some *abuelas*, or grandmothers, brush a live dove on family members to absorb their worries. The eldest son releases the dove so that it carries the worries away.

Worshipers dressed all in white sing and dance at a MITA service in Hato Rey, the main downtown business district of San Juan.

 # A time to celebrate

People in Puerto Rico and the United States celebrate many of the same holidays. Martin Luther King Jr. Day, on the third Monday in January, honors the minister and **civil rights** leader. Washington Day, on the third Monday in February, honors George Washington, the first president of the United States. Independence Day, on July 4, celebrates the United States' independence from England in 1776. Thanksgiving, on the fourth Thursday of November, celebrates the harvest and other blessings of the past year. Puerto Ricans often add their own traditions to these holidays. For example, they eat turkeys on Thanksgiving seasoned with *adobo*, a paste made from garlic, vinegar, peppercorns, and parsley or oregano.

(top) Hundreds of students sing the United States national anthem at an Independence Day celebration on July 4. Independence Day is Puerto Rico's national holiday.

Puerto Rican holidays

Puerto Ricans celebrate festivals that mark important events in their history and that remember their heroes. Luis Muñoz Rivera Day, on July 17, honors the birthday of the popular leader. Eugenio María de Hostos Day, on January 11, remembers the political **activist** and writer who helped end slavery in Puerto Rico. People also celebrate the end of slavery on March 11 with parades and tributes to those who were slaves and to their **descendants**.

On July 25, Puerto Ricans celebrate the day in 1952 when they adopted their first constitution as a commonwealth. Those who want their country's independence from the United States hold protests instead. Puerto Ricans on the island and in the United States also celebrate *El Grito de Lares* on September 23. It marks the anniversary of the day that rebels declared Puerto Rican independence from Spain. The largest celebration is in Lares, where people reenact the rebellion in the main *plaza*.

Dancers perform a traditional Spanish dance, called the flamenco, at a Christmas celebration. Flamenco dancers tap their heels to the beat and use their hands to clap, snap, and play small, wooden instruments called castanets, which make a clicking sound.

Las Navidades

Weeks before Christmas, Puerto Ricans decorate their homes with lights, Christmas trees, and *nacimientos*, or Nativity scenes, which show the story of Jesus' birth. *Las Navidades* begins on December 15 and continues until Three Kings Day on January 6. In the evenings, *plazas* are filled with people listening to *villancios*, or carolers. *Villancios* also sing at special gatherings called *parrandas*. On Christmas Day, children open presents from San Nicolás, or Saint Nicolas. Family and friends gather for a feast that includes *léchon asado*, or roast suckling pig, chicken, rice, and pigeon peas.

A young boy dressed as one of the three wise men prepares for a parade on Three Kings Day.

After Christmas

Christmas celebrations continue on December 28 with *Dia de los Inocentes*, or "Day of the Innocents." On that day, people remember the Bible story about King Herod, who killed all the male children in Bethlehem under the age of two because he wanted to make sure that the baby Jesus was dead. He thought that Jesus threatened his rule. Puerto Ricans remember *Dia de los Inocentes* by dressing up as Herod's soldiers and going from house to house to "kidnap" the eldest sons. The boys are eventually returned to their homes, where a large party awaits them. Some people no longer celebrate *Dia de los Inocentes* with a kidnapping and party. Instead, they play tricks on one another, like on April Fool's Day.

Three Kings Day

Three Kings Day, on January 6, celebrates the three kings, or wise men, who brought the baby Jesus gifts after he was born. On the evening of January 5, children leave fresh grass in shoe boxes for the kings' camels. The following morning, they eagerly open the gifts that the kings left them. A special tradition takes place in the old part of San Juan. People pray at the statues of the three kings outside the Capitol, where the government meets.

Saints' days

The Feast of San Juan Bautista, on June 24, celebrates Puerto Rico's patron saint. A patron saint is believed to protect people or places from harm. It is said that at the stroke of midnight, San Juan Bautista, or Saint John the Baptist, blesses the water around Puerto Rico. At beaches across the country, people walk into the ocean backward in the hope that it will bring them health, luck, money, and success.

Every Puerto Rican city has a patron saint. The saint is honored each year with a parade, feasts, dances in the *plaza*, musical performances, and fairs. The patron saint of Hormigueros, in the southwest, is Saint Monserrate. Thousands of **pilgrims** in Hormigueros celebrate the saint's day, on September 8, by climbing the steps of the Cathedral of Our Lady of Monserrate on their knees as a way of asking forgiveness for their sins.

A large statue of the Virgin Mary is pulled on a colorful float for a saint's day parade.

The feast of Santiago Apostol

There are different stories about the origin of the feast of Santiago Apostol, which takes place on July 25. The best-known story tells of a battle between the Spanish and the Moors, a group of **Muslims** who invaded Spain in the 800s. According to legend, the Spanish were losing a battle against the Moors when Santiago, or Saint James, appeared and helped them win. After that, Spanish soldiers called on the saint to give them strength during battles. When the Spanish came to Puerto Rico, they asked for Santiago's help in fighting against the Carib. Many Puerto Ricans adopted the belief in Santiago's powers.

Loíza Aldea holds a large parade to celebrate Santiago Apostol during which people in costume ride on floats.

Celebrating Santiago Apostol

Today, several cities celebrate the feast of Santiago Apostol. One of the largest celebrations takes place in the northeastern town of Loíza Aldea, where people wear colorful masks made from coconuts. Some masks represent the Spanish soldiers, while others represent the Moors. Scary-looking masks, called *vejigantes*, represent the Moors.

Carnaval

People wear *vejigante* masks at other Puerto Rican festivals, including *Carnaval*. *Carnaval* is the last celebration before Lent, a solemn six-week period before Easter. During Lent, Christians give up certain foods and drinks to remember the sacrifices that Jesus made.

Ponce holds one of the largest *Carnaval* celebrations in Puerto Rico. People dress up in costumes that are yellow and red or red and black. Yellow and red represent Spain, and red and black represent Ponce. The *vejigante* masks that people wear often show the West African influence in Puerto Rico. Slaves brought from West Africa made masks that looked like *vejigante* masks, but they were really masks of African gods and goddesses, who they were forbidden from worshiping.

People in Ponce parade through the streets wearing vejigante masks and throwing vejigas, or brightly painted pigs' bladders, at one another to scare each other into behaving during Lent. Some maskmakers in Ponce have become famous for their colorful or scary designs.

Harvest festivals

Puerto Ricans hold festivals to celebrate their bountiful harvests. The towns of Yauco and Maricao, in the southwest, hold coffee harvest festivals in February; San Germán, in the southwest, celebrates the sugar cane harvest in April; and, in late October, Corozal, in northcentral Puerto Rico, celebrates the harvest of plantains, which are a type of banana. At each festival, there are parades, fireworks, and tables full of food and drinks made from the harvested crop.

People wear large papier-mâché masks in a parade during the Maricao Coffee Festival.

Sing and dance

Music plays in shops, cafés, markets, and *plazas* throughout Puerto Rico. The Taíno and West Africans introduced many **percussion** instruments heard in these songs to other Puerto Ricans. The Taíno played drums made of hollowed out tree trunks; *maracas*, made of **gourds** filled with beans or stones; and *güiros*, which are gourds carved with notches. When you draw a stick across the notches, it creates a scratching sound. People of West African origin also played drums made of hollowed out logs, such as *congas* and *tambors*, as well as *palitos*, which are two sticks rapped against one another.

The *bomba*

The *bomba* is a lively type of Puerto Rican music and dance that West African slaves introduced to the country. Musicians play various drums, as well as *maracas* and *palitos*, while pairs of dancers move to the beat. The faster musicians play, the faster dancers dance, and the faster dancers dance, the faster musicians play. The drum beats and dance steps get more and more complicated as the song goes on.

The *plena*

The *plena* is a type of folk music in which a soloist and chorus sing back and forth to one another in a call and response pattern. Dancers sometimes join in the fun. They are accompanied by musicians playing horns, guitars, and percussion instruments, such as *maracas* and *panderetas*, or *panderos*, which look like tambourines without cymbals. It is believed that West African slaves working on sugar cane plantations were the first people to sing *plena* songs. The songs told of their daily struggles. *Plena* songs still tell about Puerto Ricans' difficult lives, but they also tell stories from the news or silly, made-up tales.

Décimas

In another traditional song, the *décima*, singers are accompanied by musicians playing two-, four-, or six-stringed guitars. The *décima* is based on Spanish **ballads** written in very complicated rhyming patterns. The ballads told stories of love, heroes, and daily life. In Puerto Rico, these songs became rhyming contests between *jíbaros*, who were escaped Taíno and West African slaves living in the hills and countryside. A singer sings a rhyming verse that tells a far-fetched adventure story. The next singer's rhyming verse is even more ridiculous than the first. The singers exchange verses until one of them runs out of ideas.

Singers and dancers dressed in costumes decorated with the pattern of the Puerto Rican flag perform a bomba in a plaza in San Juan. The dancers try to keep up with the lively rhythms that the musicians play on drums and maracas.

A music group playing six-stringed and eleven-stringed guitars sings a décima *at a celebration in Carolina, in the northeast.*

Danza

Many Puerto Rican dances come from Spanish styles of dance. The *danza* is a ballroom dance that is sometimes slow and romantic, and sometimes fast and lively. It is based on a Spanish dance from the 1800s called the *contradanza*. During the *contradanza*, a *bastonero*, who was like a director, decided how many couples would dance and where each pair would be positioned. The first couple performed complicated steps and the other dancers tried to copy their steps. Arguments often broke out when the imitations were not perfect. After Cuban immigrants arrived in Puerto Rico in the mid 1840s, they replaced the *contredanza* with a dance called *la habana*, in which couples had more freedom to move the way they wanted. At first, people danced to Cuban music, then Puerto Ricans composed their own music with their own sounds. This music became the *danza*. One of the greatest *danza* composers was Juan Morel Campos (1857–1896), who wrote more than 300 *danzas*. Puerto Rico's most popular *danza* is *La Borinqueña*, the country's national anthem.

A dancer wearing a colorful skirt is whirled around by her partner during a lively danza.

19

Tito Puente played many instruments, including the timbales, which is a combination of two drums, two cowbells, cymbals, and a wooden block, and the vibraphone, which looks like a xylophone, but has pedals like a piano that hold the vibrating notes for a long time.

Popular music

Musicians from Puerto Rico and from the United States who are of Puerto Rican descent have made Latin American music popular around the world. José Feliciano (1945–) was born in Lares. He is best known for playing the acoustic guitar on songs that combine classical music with Caribbean rhythms. Ricky Martin (1971–) is from San Juan. At the age of twelve, he became popular as a member of the Puerto Rican band Menudo, and then went on to a successful solo career. Jennifer Lopez (1970–) is a singer, dancer, and actor born in New York City to Puerto Rican parents. Marc Anthony (1968–) was also born in New York City. He is a singer, known for his *salsa* songs, and an actor.

Salsa

Salsa music is a blend of African rhythms, Caribbean melodies, and jazz music. Its name is translated as "sauce," which describes the spicy flavor of the music. *Salsa* was made popular in the 1950s by Tito Puente (1923–2000), a composer, bandleader, and percussionist who was born in New York City to Puerto Rican immigrants. Today, the *salsa* is the most widely heard music in Puerto Rico.

Classical music

Musicians such as Pablo Casals (1876–1973) drew attention to classical music in Puerto Rico. Pablo Casals was a cellist who grew up in Spain, but moved to Puerto Rico, where his mother was born, at the age of 81. Once there, he began a festival to showcase musicians from Puerto Rico and around the world. Casals founded a music conservatory in Puerto Rico where people study music, and he started a symphony orchestra.

Ricky Martin performs at a concert in Bayamón, which is part of Metropolitan San Juan.

Puerto Rico has a long history of painting, sculpture, and **folk art** that dates back to Taíno carvings of symbols and figures on stone and wood. Today, Puerto Rico's art shows the influences of all the people who live in the country.

José Campeche

José Campeche (1752–1809) was one of Puerto Rico's first well-known artists, as well as a musician and **architect**. Many of his paintings and sculptures show people in a very detailed, realistic way, and reflect his strong Roman Catholic background. Campeche used paints that he made himself from the juices of plants and flowers. As a result, the colors of his work are very different from the colors that other artists used.

Francisco Oller y Cestero's painting The Student *shows a student with his tutor. The painting hangs in the Museum of Puerto Rican Art in Santurce, a suburb of San Juan.*

Francisco Oller y Cestero

Francisco Oller y Cestero (1833–1917) painted both in impressionistic and realistic styles. Impressionists use bright colors and blurry shapes to portray an impression of their subjects, while realist painters focus on small details that make their paintings look true to life. Among Cestero's realistic paintings are works that show scenes of slavery, poverty, and other problems in society. Cestero also painted many scenes of Puerto Rico's natural beauty.

José Campeche's painting San Juan Nepomuceno *shows a saint studying a cross, which is a religious symbol for Jesus Christ.*

Other early artists

In the early 1900s, Ramon Frade (1875–1954) and Miguel Pou (1880–1968) created paintings that showed Puerto Ricans' difficult lives. In Frade's painting *El pan Nuestro de Cada Día*, a *jíbaro*, or peasant farmer, carries a heavy bunch of bananas, his face full of sadness because of the hardships of his life. *The Promise*, by Pou, shows a peasant woman holding a saint's picture. Even though she has few belongings, she still has faith.

Modern artists

In the 1960s, artists of Puerto Rican background living in the United States began to experiment with new styles of art. Silk-screening, printing, woodcutting, and linocutting were different ways of applying ink to cloth, wood, paper, or canvas. Antonio Martorell (1939–) created woodcuts of the letters of the alphabet, then he printed the letters on fabrics of all colors and textures. Students from a public school in New York City helped him by posing in the shape of the letters. Martorell has also created many installations, which are works of art designed for a particular setting. For example, he filled a gallery with flowers and trees made of all kinds of cardboard boxes.

Antonio Martorell displays one of his installation pieces at the Museo de Arte e Historia in San Juan. The installation is a cart that Martorell decorated with colorful paint, cardboard, ribbon, and trim.

Murals showing community spirit, activities, and history are painted on walls and the sides of buildings in some neighborhoods of San Juan.

Folk art

Beautiful hammocks and tatted cloths hang in markets throughout Puerto Rico. Tatting is a way of knotting twine into different patterns, like crocheting, and is often used to make borders for hammocks. These borders are called *mundillos*. Folk artists also make detailed carvings of saints and other people from the Bible. Statues of saints are called *santos*. They are often decorated with *milagros*, or "miracles," which are small metal charms in the shape of body parts that people believe the saint can heal. *Vejigante* masks are a type of Puerto Rican folk art influenced by West African culture. The masks originally looked like devils, but are now also shaped like sheep, pigs, donkeys, and other animals.

Some vejigante masks take months to make. Craftspeople who make vejigantes must study the art of maskmaking for years.

To make a lace mundillo, a girl ties threads wrapped around different bobbins into tiny knots. Pins separating the threads hold the lace in place.

Sports and pastimes

Juan "Chi Chi" Rodriguez (1935–) learned to play golf by hitting cans with clubs made from tree branches. He has won many regular Professional Golfers' Association (PGA) tournaments and Senior PGA tournaments.

Puerto Ricans love playing baseball and basketball, swimming and riding bicycles, and going for leisurely *paseos*, or strolls, in *plazas*. Children play games such as *El Gato y el Raton*, or "the Cat and the Mouse." To play the game, they walk or skip around in a circle while singing a song. In the meantime, one child, the mouse, stands in the center of the circle, while another child, the cat, stands on the outside. The cat has to try to get inside the circle to trap the mouse.

Baseball

In parks and on streets throughout Puerto Rico, children play baseball, the island's national sport. Many players on Major League teams, including Roberto Alomar, Juan González, and Ivan Rodriguez, are from Puerto Rico. Roberto Clemente (1934–1972) was Puerto Rico's best-loved baseball player. In 1955, Clemente joined the Pittsburgh Pirates, a team he played with for

eighteen years. He helped the Pirates win two World Series, in 1960 and 1971, and was named most valuable player of the 1971 series. Clemente, who was also known for his **humanitarian** efforts, died in a plane crash. He was on his way to deliver medical supplies, food, and clothing to victims of an earthquake in Nicaragua.

Cockfighting

Cockfighting is a sport that is banned in many parts of the world because people object to the cruel treatment of the roosters that are fighting, but it is still popular in Puerto Rico. Roosters are specially raised to fight one another, often slashing each other with razors or spurs on their feet. People gather in *galleras*, or rings, to watch the fights, and bet on which bird will win.

Horse racing

Watching Paso Fino horses race in San Juan is a favorite Puerto Rican pastime. Paso Fino horses are raised in Arenales, in the northwest; in Coamo, in the south; and on the island of Vieques. Christopher Columbus first brought the horses from Spain. They were named *los caballos de paso fino*, or "the horses with the fine step," because of the very even way in which they walk.

Competitors demonstrate the different steps their Paso Fino horses can do at a fair in Ponce.

Roberto Clemente was a left fielder who won the National League batting title four times and the Golden Glove award twelve times.

Taíno ball games

The Taíno people played a fast-paced ball game called *batey* on large rectangular courts. Two teams competed against one another. The object of the game was to score a goal by getting the ball, called a *batu*, to the opposite end of the court. Players could not touch the ball with their hands. Instead, they kicked the ball or bounced it off another player's feet, legs, or shoulders. Some even bounced the ball off stone belts, called belt bats, that players wore around their waists. The balls were very heavy and many people were injured, or even killed, during *batey* games.

A group of men play a game called palo encebado, *or "greasy pole." The object of the game is to get to the top of a tall pole covered in grease by climbing on the shoulders and backs of your opponents. At the top of the pole is a prize, which is usually a small sack filled with money.*

Different languages

Puerto Rico's two official languages are Spanish and English, so you might hear people greeting each other with both "*Hola*" and "Hello." Spanish became Puerto Rico's main language during Spain's rule. Over time, people in Puerto Rico began to speak a version of Spanish that had a slightly different accent, different pronunciation, and different vocabulary than the Spanish spoken in Spain.

Puerto Rican Spanish

Nearly 500 words in Puerto Rican Spanish come from the Taíno language, including *colibrí*, which means "hummingbird," *mime*, which is a small fly, and *cacique*, which is a chief or leader. Some Taíno words have found their way into English. *Hamaca* is "hammock" and *canoa* is "canoe." The word *iguana* comes from Taíno and is used in both Spanish and English.

Yoruba, a language that the West African slaves brought to Puerto Rico, has also influenced Puerto Rican Spanish. Words such as *quimbombo*, which is the vegetable "okra," and *gueneo*, which means "banana," are Yoruba words.

Language in school

In the 1800s, most Puerto Rican children went to small community schools, studied at home with their families, or had no education at all. Instead, they worked on their families' farms or in their families' businesses. When the United States took over the country, it introduced the public school system. Every child was guaranteed a free education, but classes had to be taught in English. This presented a problem since most students and teachers spoke Spanish.

In 1948, the United States government gave Puerto Ricans control of their education system. Puerto Ricans could decide what subjects to teach and in what language to teach them. Most classes were taught in Spanish, but children had to learn English as well. Today, students learn both languages in school.

Children use computer programs in school that teach them to read in Spanish and English.

English	Spanish
Hello.	Hola.
Goodbye.	Adios.
Please.	Por favor.
Thank you.	Gracias.
You're welcome.	De nada.
Good morning.	Buenas dias.
Good night.	Buenas noches.
See you later.	Hasta luego.
Have a nice day.	Que tenga un buen dia.
Breakfast.	Desayunar.
Lunch.	Comer.
Dinner.	Cenar.
Happy birthday.	Feliz cumpleaños.
Best wishes.	Felicidades.
Pleased to meet you.	Encantado.

Puerto Ricans returning to the island after many years in the United States are more comfortable with English than Spanish. These students practice Spanish by reading books from the library.

Spanglish

Many Puerto Ricans in the United States speak Spanglish, a mix of Spanish and English. Some words in Spanglish are English words pronounced with a Spanish accent. *Lonch* is "lunch." *Oben* is "oven." *Winshiwaipers* are "windshield wipers." Other Spanglish words are actual words in Spanish, but they mean something different. For example, the Spanglish word *mayor* means "mayor" in English and "larger" in Spanish.

Some people of Puerto Rican background frown on Spanglish because they think that it threatens their Spanish heritage. Others think Spanglish is a way for Puerto Ricans to show pride in their Spanish and English backgrounds.

 # In print and on film

The earliest known stories from Puerto Rico were Taíno creation stories, which told how the world came to be. Other Taíno stories taught people lessons about how they should live. The Taíno did not have a written language, so they passed their stories from generation to generation by word of mouth. When the Spanish came to Puerto Rico, they wrote down some Taíno stories that survive today.

The Spanish and West Africans introduced new folktales and legends to Puerto Rico. Literature eventually began to deal with politics, such as, what it meant to be Puerto Rican. Manuel A. Alonso (1822–1889) was a poet who wrote about the struggles of Puerto Ricans. His poetry collection *El Jíbaro* is about the poor treatment of the country's peasants and farmers.

Look in a book

In the 1890s, novels gained popularity. Manuel Zeno Gandia (1855–1930) wrote *La Charca*, which means *Stagnant Pool*. The book contrasts Puerto Rico's natural beauty with the poor conditions of the people living there. Poetry continued to be important. Luis Llórens Torres (1887–1945) wrote poems about *"criollismo,"* a type of nationalism that celebrates the customs and traditions of Puerto Ricans. His collections include *Alturas de América*, or *Heights of America*.

(top) Performers prepare to reenact a Taíno story about the hummingbird, which the Taíno called guaracacigaba, or "rays of the sun." According to legend, hummingbirds were once tiny flies that glowed in the night sky. They were changed into beautiful birds and given shiny colors by the god of the sun so they could glow during the day.

Children in Puerto Rico read different types of books. Some are American stories, some are Spanish folktales, and some are Puerto Rican legends.

Modern writers

Julia de Burgos (1914–1953) was a poet whose work combined her experiences with love and loneliness with her political beliefs, such as Puerto Rico's right to independence. René Marqués (1919–1979) was a novelist and playwright. His play *La Carreta*, or *The Oxcart*, tells of the struggles of a Puerto Rican family adjusting to a new life in the United States. Piri Thomas (1928–) was born in New York City to Puerto Rican and Cuban parents. In his autobiography *Down These Mean Streets*, he describes the difficulties he experienced growing up as a Puerto Rican and Cuban in New York.

Actress Rita Moreno has won several lifetime achievement awards for her work on stage, in film, and on television.

Theater

Actors from Puerto Rico have found fame around the world. José Ferrer (1912–1992) won an Academy Award in 1950 for his role in the movie *Cyrano de Bergerac*. Rita Moreno (1931–) has won all the major entertainment awards in the United States — an Oscar, Emmy, Grammy, and Tony. She has appeared in many plays and films, including the movie version of *West Side Story*. *The Addams Family* movie starred another Puerto Rican actor named Raúl Julia (1940–1994), who was also known for his role in *Kiss of the Spider Woman*.

Puerto Rican actor Raúl Julia and American actress Anjelica Huston play the roles of Gomez and Morticia Addams in the movie The Addams Family.

Armando has trouble concentrating in school the day before he and his family leave for Ponce. Armando goes to a public school in San Juan.

It was dawn in San Juan, and Armando leaped out of bed. He and his parents were flying to Ponce, on the other side of the island, where his *tía*, or aunt, *tío*, or uncle, and *primas*, or cousins, lived. Armando was even more excited because it was *Carnaval* in Ponce. He couldn't wait to see the parade of people dressed up in their colorful costumes, even those wearing frightening *vejigantes* masks.

Armando crept down the hallway and into the kitchen, where his mother was making herself a warm cup of *café con leche*, or coffee mixed with milk.

"Mama, what are you doing home so early?" Armando's mother works the overnight shift at a factory that manufactures computers. She does not usually get home until after Armando leaves for school.

Armando's mother laughed. "I should ask why you are up already," and she kissed him on the forehead. "My supervisor let me leave a little early because she knew we were flying to Ponce."

"I was too excited to sleep," Armando said. "I can't wait to get to Ponce to see Tía Nina, Tío Benigno, Emelia, and Mallorie."

Armando and his mother made a large breakfast of eggs and leftover rice and beans with *sofrito*. The *sofrito*, a sauce made from bacon, ham, tomatoes, garlic, onions, chilies, coriander, and other spices, was delicious.

As they prepared the food, Armando thought about how much fun he had the last time he was in Ponce. His *tía* and *tío* took him and his *primas* to the Parque de Bombas, which was a red and black museum filled with old fire trucks. They also went to the Museo del Arte de Ponce, where they saw paintings by famous Puerto Rican artists, including José Campeche, Francisco Oller y Cestero, and Antonio Martorell.

The flight from San Juan to Ponce took less than an hour. After a short taxi ride, Armando and his parents were at his aunt, uncle, and cousins' house.

"*Hola!*" called out Tío Benigno as he opened the door. "Come in. Come in. Once you're settled, we have a surprise for you. We hope you like *léchon asado*."

"Who doesn't?" Armando exclaimed. "I thought we only ate roasted pig on special occasions like Christmas."

"This is a special occasion," Tía Nina smiled. "After we eat, we'll go to the *plaza* for the *Carnaval* celebrations."

Just before it was time to leave, Emelia motioned to Armando, "Come to my room. I want to show you something."

Armando gasped as Emelia opened her closet door. Behind it was a large, colorful mask with horns and terrible-looking teeth. It was a *vejigante*.

"Papa says that I can wear this tonight," Emelia explained.

"I'm still too young to dress up in a *vejigante* mask," Mallorie added, "but in a few years I will have a mask of my own."

Just then, Tía Nina called the children. "It's time to go, or we'll be late."

*Emelia and Tío Benigno, **wearing their** vejigante **masks and vibrant costumes, are excited to begin the** Carnaval **parade.***

The Parque de Bombas, in Ponce, is a museum with old fire engines and firefighting equipment.

"See you at the parade," Emelia said. "I'm going to put on my mask, then Papa and I will go to the *plaza* together."

"*Hasta luego*," Armando said. "Try not to scare me and Mallorie too much."

Emelia laughed as Armando and Mallorie got ready to begin their *Carnaval* celebrations.

Glossary

activist A person who works to change other people's ideas and actions about an important cause

altar A table or stand used for religious ceremonies

architect A designer of buildings

ballad A love song

barren Unable to produce crops or vegetation

civil rights The basic rights of a person

colonist A person who lives on a settlement controlled by a distant country

denomination An organized religious group within a faith

descendant A person who can trace his or her family roots to a certain family or group

discrimination Treating people unfairly because of race, religion, gender, or other factors

economic Dealing with the way a country organizes and manages its business, industries, and money

folk art Art that reflects the culture of a country or group of people

fortification A building that has been strengthened or secured to protect it from invasion and attack

gourd The hard-shelled fruit of certain vines, which is dried and used to make cups, bowls, and musical instruments

humanitarian Helping other people

Kardecism A religion whose followers believe that people can communicate with the spirits of those who died. They also believe in reincarnation, or being born over again.

legislature The group of people who make laws for a country

manioc A starchy root vegetable that is shaped like a carrot

Muslim A person who believes in Islam, a religion based on the teachings of God, whom Muslims call Allah, and his prophet Muhammad

nationalist Wanting independence for one's country

percussion Relating to an instrument that produces sound when one object strikes another, such as a drum

pilgrim A person who makes a religious journey to a sacred place

plain A large area of flat land

plantation A large farm on which crops such as cotton and sugar are grown

plaza A public square

republic A country led by an elected government

ritual A religious ceremony in which steps must be followed in a certain order

Index